The Basic Essentials of
CANOE PADDLING

by Harry Roberts

illustration assistance by
Jamie Bastian

ICS BOOKS, Inc.
Merrillville, Indiana

THE BASIC ESSENTIALS OF CANOE PADDLING

10 9 8 7 6 5 4 3 2 1

Printed in U.S.A.

Dedication

There are literally hundreds of paddlers to whom this book should be dedicated, and they all know who they are, and why this book should be dedicated to them. All but two of them, that is.

So, this book is for Gus Chutorash, for many years the director of the Detroit Area Council of the Boy Scouts of America's Cole Canoe Base and one of the kindest, most thoughtful men in the world, who had faith that a skinny, graying writer could teach his waterfront people how to teach paddling in a way that would meet with more success than the traditional way, and who stuck with it in the face of a lot of "experts" who told him otherwise.

And it's also for Lisa Knox, one of Gus's waterfront water rats, whom I've watched with amazement as she grew from a zingy kid who loved to paddle into an environmental scientist, a fine instructor of paddlesport, the first female program director for a major Boy Scout Camp in history, and a lovely, gracious young woman.

Gus, Lisa, you've lit up the dark corners in a whole lot of lives, including mine. Thanks.

Published by:

ICS Books, Inc.
1370 E. 86th Place
Merrillville, IN 46410
800/541-7323

Library of Congress Cataloging-in-Publication Data

Roberts, Harry.
    The basic essentials of canoe paddling / by Harry Roberts.
        p.   cm. -- (Basic essentials series)
    Includes index.
    ISBN 0-934802-68-8 : $4.95
    1. Canoes and canoeing.   I. Title.
GV783.R6 1992
797.1 ' 22--dc20

90-25773
CIP

TABLE OF CONTENTS

INTRODUCTION

This book's about paddling. It's not about selecting a canoe. It's not about tents or sleeping bags or cooking gear or portage packs. It's about paddling. Because paddling is, in my experience, the part of canoeing that's frequently forgotten, even though it's the part of canoeing that can make or break your trip.

There's a popular notion that anybody can paddle. Let's rephrase that. Anybody can be taught to paddle. Paddle well, paddle easily, paddle efficiently, paddle in control, and paddle safely.

But why bother, you say? Millions of people go canoeing every weekend and seem to be having a good time, and most of them don't paddle well. Why bother?

Well—are they having a good time? If they were, they'd be out on the water next week; maybe even out on the water the next day, in their own canoe. The fact is that most have a good time swimming, or fishing, or splashing water and tipping over, or, in what's come to be a noxious tradition on many waterways, getting drunk and rowdy. A few enjoy watching birds, sensing the constant variations of light dancing on the water, and slipping into a oneness with the natural world. But very few enjoy paddling. Very few get involved in the feel of a good canoe slipping quickly, easily and powerfully through the water under perfect and nearly unconscious control. Very few paddle well enough to be free to absorb the world around them without worrying about wind, waves, current and even a fundamental thing like keeping the boat going straight. In simple terms, learning to paddle well lets you enjoy canoeing more. Who knows? You might even find yourself catching an hour on the water every day after dinner! Most of us live close enough to a paddleable waterway to do just that. But you'll never do that unless you enjoy paddling—the art and craft of making a canoe do exactly what you want it to do when you want it to.

So—we'll be talking together about the easiest way to learn to paddle. And I mean "easiest." This isn't the School of One Thousand Strokes And A Stroke! It's a couple of strokes—but strokes learned so well that you don't have to think about them. And before we start, I'd like to ask you one favor. This is a contemporary approach to paddling. If you've learned a bit about paddling in the past—as I did—you'll be confused by some of what you'll read. The paddle size and design I'll recommend won't look much like what you're familiar with. You'll be told that it's not only okay to sit in a canoe—you'll be told that it's generally preferable. And you'll be told that switching sides when you paddle is a sign of artistry, not a sign of terminal ineptitude.

This is a new way to paddle; new at least to a lot of folks. It s fancy name is North American Touring Technique, and I confess I coined that name for it. Marathon racers—those men and women who paddle long distances in skinny canoes at average speeds of over seven miles per hour on dead flat water—call it "sit-and-switch." It's an accurate name. You do sit in the canoe, and you switch sides. You switch sides to aid in directional control, to permit more powerful boat handling strokes, and to distribute the effort over all muscle groups. But "sit-and-switch" is an unlovely phrase at best, evoking memories of parental discipline rather than thoughts of clear water and the sound of a canoe running at speed. Clearly, the name needed some gussying up. So—it became North American Touring Technique, or NATT for short.

The name's a mouthful. And I promise I won't use it again until the last chapter in the book. But when you start paddling this way, and you just plain flat-out blow the rails off your companions and get to the takeout so far ahead of them that you were able to read the first half of *Anna Karenina* and still add three birds to your life list, I'd appreciate it if you'd tell your friends the full name for the way you paddle. It'd make me feel good. It really would.

And it'd make me feel good to see the looks of astonishment on the faces of your paddling buddies when you and your partner just take off and leave them, with smiles on your faces and a notable absence of sweat on your brows. I won't be there, of course. But I've seen that look enough to know what it is——and I'm smiling already.

I've run off at the mouth enough. Zip up your PFD and let's go paddling!

1. STARTING RIGHT

T'ang said to Baso, "How is it that water, which has no bones, can support a ship of 1,000 tons?"

Baso replied, "There's no water here, and no ship. What can I tell you?"

I can only assume you already have a canoe, and a partner who's willing to forgive you your trespasses. If you don't, I'd need a book of about this size to talk about the process of selecting a canoe. Yeah; there are that many choices, and designs are subtle. But, as we don't have that other book, I'll have to assume that you own a canoe, and that your primary intent is to take that canoe somewhere and look at something. If you lust for the thrill of playing in whitewater, you've bought the wrong book. If you drool over sea kayaks, you've bought the wrong book. What can I tell you?

Your Paddle

This probably isn't the paddle you have. If it isn't, go get one. The paddle you should have for going somewhere in a canoe and maintaining a nicety of both control and efficiency is a "bent shaft paddle" of approximately 15 degrees (your outfitter will know what you mean when you tell him you want a 15 degree bent shaft), with a blade width of, preferably, no more than 8 inches and a blade length of 18-20 inches. I insist that the shaft be oval rather than round, and that

1

the grip—the knob on the top of the shaft—is what's generally called a "palm grip." Why the bent shaft paddle of about 15 degrees? Simple. A paddle functions efficiently within a range of 15 degrees to either side of vertical. Build in the angle to begin with, and you can use a shorter, less tiring stroke with a shorter, lighter, handier paddle. Why the relatively narrow blade? Simple. It's less tiring to take more light, easy strokes than fewer humongous strokes. Also, the smaller blade won't twist in your hand as easily under power. Why the oval shaft and the modified palm grip? Simple. Increased comfort and control.

Now, how do we fit this strange tool? Here's how. Sit on a flat chair or bench. Turn the paddle upside-down, and place the handle between your legs, the shaft pointing straight up. If you're sitting erect, your nose should touch the throat of the paddle—that place on the paddle where you can't tell whether it's the blade or the shaft. That measurement, from bench to nose, is called *Base Shaft Length*. I don't know what canoe you're paddling but unless it's a big tripping boat with a flared bow, a bent shaft paddle with a shaft length of that measurement will do you nicely. If you paddle a big tripper, one that's 25 inches wide or more from rail to rail at the front of the bow seat, consider a stick with a shaft length an inch or two longer. If, in spite of my honest, open face and reputation for trustworthiness, you prefer a straight shaft paddle because some guru told you you needed one to better control the canoe, add four inches to that base shaft length—or six if you paddle a big boat.

Okay. I brought up the subject of control, so I'd best deal with it right now. If you're paddling whitewater—and that doesn't mean "running a rapid," it means "playing" a rapid—I'm quick to concede that the reversing strokes you'll be using and the pry strokes you'll need are better done with a straight shaft paddle. If you're a "going somewhere" paddler, you can make a canoe do anything you need it to do with a bent shaft. And for probably 99 percent of your paddling, you can do it better and more efficiently. If you couldn't, the folks who paddle marathon canoe races and the folks who race open boats in downriver events in whitewater would be using straight shaft paddles. They don't.

So much for the paddle, almost. If you're buying paddles, may I suggest that a degree of equivalency be maintained between what the bow paddler gets and what the stern paddler gets? I've been in this game a long time, and all too often I've seen The Captain of the Ship

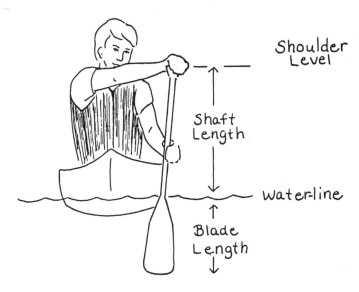

Figure 1-1 This is the body position you should be in when your paddle is properly sized. Note that *shaft length* is the critical dimension

buy himself the latest and lightest, and get the First Mate (otherwise known as wife, because no girlfriend would put up with such nonsense) a heavy, clumsy club that he wouldn't use as a spare, because "it's good enough". Get paddles that feel good and look good, and you'll use them more. Betcha!

Your Life Jacket (PFD)

Every state mandates that you have a U.S. Coast Guard approved PFD (Personal Flotation Device) on board for each passenger. When I'm teaching, I mandate that each paddler in my class wears a PFD, and I wear one myself. Learn to paddle while wearing PFD, and you won't feel uncomfortable with one on. Yeah. I know. Paddling's a barefoot sport, a sun and sand sport, and a PFD sort of spoils the image. So does drowning. Wear the PFD. Sure, there'll be times in non-threatening, warm water on a warm day, when you can slip out of the PFD. That's a judgment call. You're just learning to paddle. You're just learning what situations are threatening and which are not. Until you know, wear the PFD all the time. If you're less than confident as a swimmer, wear the PFD all the time. It's a confidence-builder and a warm, cozy buddy when the chilly winds pick up.

What kind to get? The kind your canoe shop might call a "paddling vest." It looks like a vest made of closed-cell foam strips covered with nylon, and it has a zipper closure and a waistbelt that either ties or buckles. It should fit you comfortably; too tight is, well, too tight, and too loose means that it could ride up over your head when you least want it to. It shouldn't bite your neck, and it shouldn't bind under your arms. Your canoe shop can advise you on the fine points of fit.

A good PFD will set you back $50-$60. You can get cheap orange horsecollar PFDs for about $10. You can get flotation cushions for about the same. Either will fulfil your obligation under boating laws. So why not get them? The horsecollar fits so badly that you won't wear it, and it's of dubious value as a protective device because it leaves your back unprotected. The flotation cushion is great for lunch break, but do you really think you're going to be able to get to it if your boat overturns, or if you take a nosedive out of your boat and the wind or current blows your boat and the cushion away? Get a good PFD. Wear it. End of sermon.

Tricking Out Your Canoe

If you're not comfortable in a canoe, you won't paddle it much. And if you're neither comfortable in your canoe nor feel as if you're a part of it, you won't paddle well and easily. In general, the tweaking you do to gain comfort is the same tweaking you do to gain efficiency. Let's get to it!

First a little theory. When you plant the paddle in the water, you're pulling your backside up to it (and past it, because the canoe keeps moving after you've backed off). If your backside isn't firmly attached to the canoe, you waste a lot of effort, and you're never really comfortable in the canoe. Wasted effort and discomfort won't leave you pleading to go paddling again.

Comfort starts by padding the seat with thin closed-cell foam of the sort that go-light backpackers carry. Some folks opt for enclosing the foam in a comfy fabric. I suppose there's merit to that. But not in the damp maritime climate I live with on the shores of Lake Huron. Now, if the seat pad was detachable, you could convince me. You know; hold it in place with Velcro? Why didn't I think of that! Don't answer.

This pad not only makes the seat—bucket or bench—more comfortable, but it also provides a degree of contour to the seat that enables your backside to stay put when you're paddling. And you can help that along by remounting the canoe seats so that they are slightly (an inch is fine) higher in the back than in the front. It's called canting the seat, and it gives you something to push against. Push against? Yep; push against—because your feet will be braced against some sort of immovable object called, not surprisingly, a footbrace. This might be the flotation chamber for the bow paddler. For the stern paddler, it may be nothing more elaborate than a dowel rod anchored to the stern seat by parachute cord. It may be a telescoping footbrace that can be instantly adjusted for length—or anything in between.

The dowel rod footbrace has some drawbacks. There is no question whatever that you could get tangled up in the chute cord that affixes it to the seat and to the stern intermediate thwart if you dumped the boat. The odds are against it, but it could happen.

If your seat is placed so low that you bump your armpits against the rails, raise the seat. If the seat is so high that you feel uncomfortable in the canoe, lower the seat. If the canoe doesn't ride level in the water with you and your partner in it, move the bow seat forward or aft to make the boat trim; move the stern seat too if you must. If you want to get fancy—or just plain do the job right to begin with—mount a sliding seat in the bow. If that doesn't give you a level trim, mount a stern slider as well. If there's a fair weight discrepancy between you and your partner, go directly to the bow and stern slider setup, or rig the canoe in such a way as you can to mount an extra set of seats placed in such a way as to permit you to switch places.

Switch places? Isn't that heresy? Won't The Grand Inquisitor step from the pages of *The Brothers Karamazov* and grill me about my paddling faith? Yes and probably. If you paddle with this style, you should be able to paddle bow and stern with anybody who paddles this style. You'll be able to paddle from either side with aplomb. And if you're used to being the Captain sitting in the stern and barking out orders to the Mate, you're in for a rude awakening. A pleasant awakening, actually. It's easy to flip a bass bug at a log when you're in the bow! (Darn! Don't let Molly read this, or I'll be back in the stern again!)

Anyway, set the boat up so you can trim it level without gear, so you can keep your butt fixed in place when you're working, and so you have somewhere to plant your feet. If you can do it, fine. If you can't, go to your friendly local canoe dealer and solicit his help. While you're there, you might ask him why in hell he didn't sell you a boat with a bow slider and footbraces in the first place!

2. THE BASIC FORWARD STROKE

Over 95% of your paddle strokes will be made to move your canoe in a straight line, and over 95% of the rest of your strokes will be simple control and turning strokes that are little more than forward strokes taken in a direction other than parallel to the keel line of your canoe. You don't have to be a rocket scientist to know that learning a good forward stroke gives you a solid foundation for virtually all of your paddling. So, let's take our paddles, and before we make a mad dash to the water with our canoe and our life jackets, let's stick a piece of tape on the back face of your paddle. That's the side of the blade that isn't used in the forward stroke. Done that? Great! Now, let's get on the water and get to it.

Getting Into Your Canoe

Oops! Forgot something. It's tough to learn a forward stroke if you tip your canoe over getting into it. And would you believe that getting into and out of a canoe is when most upsets occur? Yep. It's true. Take it to the bank. Believe me—nothing can squelch the joy of a day on the water like a thorough soaking before you even get on the water!

Canoes are stable craft. It's paddlers that make canoes unstable. Set a canoe adrift in whitewater or on a big lake when the whitecaps are rolling, and the canoe will take care of itself. Add two paddlers, and you raise the center of gravity and the roll center of the canoe, and the

6

canoe loses some of its rock-solid stability. A modicum of common sense and a pinch of learning will compensate for that once you're on the water. But going from the bank to the water is tricky. A canoe isn't very stable when its bow is on shore, its stern balanced precariously on the river bottom, and nothing but air under its middle. It also isn't very strong. Canoes are designed to be strong when they're supported by water, not when they're balanced precariously on both ends. More canoes are tipped over—and more canoes are damaged—getting in and getting out of than are damaged even on whitewater streams.

I don't want to talk this point to death. This isn't exactly a spiritual crisis we're dealing with, after all. Here's the drill. Put the entire boat in the water parallel to the shore and in water at least six inches deep. Put your paddles in the canoe where (1) you can reach them easily, and (2) you won't trip over them. With both paddlers facing the bow (the front), grasp both gunwales (rails) of the canoe to steady it. The bow paddler does this aft of the bow seat, because it's easier to keep the boat stable from that position than from further forward, because the canoe is wider and more stable at that point. The stern paddler does the same in front of the stern seat. The stern paddler enters first. Keep your seat low and your head dropped down to lower your center of gravity. The first foot in goes right smack in the middle of the canoe—right over the keel line. Swing over the near rail, still holding the rails and keeping low, put your other foot beside the first, and kneel in front of the stern seat to keep the boat firm while your bow paddler gets in, using the same method. One more time, now; hands on both rails, seat and head dropped, knees flexed, first foot goes dead in the center of the boat. When you're both seated comfortably, pick up your paddles. Your feet may be wet, but that's no big deal. The rest of you is dry, the boat isn't battered, and it's floating freely, awaiting your commands.

Now, there are fancy sculling maneuvers that you can use to move the boat into the water deep enough for paddling. And these maneuvers look sharp and make you feel good about yourself. We'll worry about them later. For now, push yourself away gently with the paddles. I promise I won't tell anybody that you did it that way if you won't tell anybody that I told you to do it.

Getting Going

You're on the water and floating free, with enough depth under the hull that you won't bash your paddle on the bottom. Great. You'll start paddling with one paddler paddling on the right side of the canoe and the other on the left side. I'll be arbitrary here, because it makes it easier for me to write about the process. The bow paddler will start on the left and the stern paddler on the right.

Okay, bow paddler, take the funny little knob on the top of the paddle shaft (it's called a "palm grip") in your right hand, and place your left hand on the paddle shaft about 2-1/2 to 3 hands' widths up the shaft from the top of the blade. Stern paddler, your left hand is on the grip and your right hand on the shaft—again, about 2-1/2 to 3 hands' widths above the blade. Some nomenclature here. The hand that's on the paddle shaft is called the "grip hand"; the hand on the grip is called the "control hand." If this is a little confusing, remember it this way: the hand on the grip is the hand that controls the angle of the paddle blade. The hand on the paddle shaft simply grips the paddle loosely. Avoid a death grip on your paddle. Hold your paddle with the same tenderness you'd use if you were handed a day-old baby.

Figure 2-1 If your grip hand is too close to the paddle blade, you can't paddle efficiently.

Now, sit erect but "easy," like a big league shortstop waiting on the pitcher to throw the ball. Rotate your upper torso a little, with your grip hand leading, and simply place the paddle in the water, with the blade vertical or nearly so and your arms nearly straight and away from your body, and rotate your upper torso back to neutral. Lift the paddle out of the water with the same forward rotation, grip hand leading, put the paddle into the water, pull yourself up to the paddle again by "unwinding" your upper body, and so on. It's a simple, repetitive move that, in a sense, keeps the shoulder of your control hand almost still and the rest of your upper body rotating around it.

Okay? Erect but not stiff? Rotating your upper body around the fixed point of the shoulder of your control hand? Rotating back to neutral and lifting the paddle out of the water with the same motion, in reverse, that put it there? Paddle blade vertical or nearly so? Good. Even if it doesn't feel good, it's a good start.

Your arms really don't do much in a good touring stroke. It's not strictly correct to say that they do nothing, but the real engine that drives the boat are the large muscle of your back, shoulders and belly. And they can drive the boat easily because your feet are planted and your backside isn't slipping, and you have a firm foundation against which to work.

Figure 2-2 Good body rotation and a minimum of forward lean. This stroke will be powerful!

Now, here's the tricksy bit. You've paddled a few strokes, and the boat is starting to move along. But it's turning to the side on which the bow paddler's paddling. And it's bobbing and diving and feeling wiggly. Let the boat glide nearly to a stop and start over again. Bow paddler, do that simple, repetitive stroke in a regular, metronomic rhythm. It needn't be fast; that comes with a lot of practice. One stroke every two seconds is just fine for starters. Stern paddler, keep your bow paddler's tempo. Put your paddle in the water at the same time, rotate your upper body through the same degree of arc, take your paddle out of the water at the same time, and so forth. Just like dancing. Uh-uh. Strike that. *Maybe.*

Interlude

Back when I was a young man in high school, dancing was a face-to-face activity, even if the sisters at the Patrician Club canteen that Vincentian Institute ran for high schoolers every Friday night did prowl the dance floor with laboratory meter sticks and ran them up and down between the couples to be sure that there was no body contact. Try as they may, the sisters never achieved ubiquity, so there was some body contact. It's difficult to dance in close proximity—a nice euphemism for dancing while both partners are hugging each other for dear life—without being aware of the location of your partner's feet, and the tempo of your partner's movement. We had to dance *together,* even if my motivation had precious little to do with what I learned in Miss Munson's Academy of Ballroom Dance. If you lacked that sensitivity to the music and your partner, you could have been the early 1950s precursor of Captain California and every young lady you asked to dance would have to immediately dash off to what they called the powder room—with two friends in tow. Now, I was tall and skinny—a geek by any standards. But I could dance. Not showily, to be sure. When the up-tempo stuff started, I found an excuse to talk with the young lady with whom I found myself. But good ol' close dancing? I could do that! And I'll bet that anybody reading this book who's past the age of forty-five can dance to slow music pretty well. Anything from an Eddy Howard ballad to "Moon River" brings back fond and not always lily-white memories. If you danced to slow music, you can damn well paddle at the same tempo as your partner!

Of course, if you're locked into playing the Marriage Game, if Dad must be the Captain and Mom must be the First Mate (or the

Galley Slave, depending on how hard a game you play), you might have trouble arriving at a mutually acceptable tempo. This is a matter for negotiation, not for ultimatums. If all else fails, try to hum the tenor soloist's line of "If I Didn't Care," or Nat King Cole's "Mona Lisa" and let pleasant memories take over.

If you're younger, and grew up courting to rock, you certainly understand dancing, but you never had the chance to work out an accommodation with a partner who was close to you. I'm sorry; I have no hints to help you. I'll just trust to your rhythmic sense and the fact that you grew up with a lot less of the "Me Tarzan, You Jane" junk than I did.

By now the old canoe should be running along pretty nicely, but it still wants to turn to the side that the bow paddler is on. That's simple physical law. If you look at a canoe with two paddlers in it, the stern paddler's paddle is farther away from the centerline of the canoe, and his/her stroke is also nearer to the canoe's center of rotation than the bow paddler's stroke. Hence, the canoe has to turn away from the stern's stroke. (Sorry, stern paddler. You're not "overpowering" your bow paddler. Unflex your biceps, spit out your chew of Red Man and testosterone, and unclench.) And the canoe will continue to turn unless you do something to stop it from turning.

Back at good old Camp Yukintipovurtu, in the days of your youth, you learned something called a J-stroke from a camp counselor who was probably bored silly, preoccupied with dreams about somebody in a red swim suit at the camp across the lake, and didn't know much about canoeing to begin with. And the old J-stroke worked, after a fashion. You had a gut feeling that it scrubbed off a lot of the canoe's speed, and was sort of like accelerating away from a stop light and stabbing the brakes at the same time, but it got you there. But that's not what you'll be doing right now. You'll be doing something else.

Think about this. If the bow paddler is paddling on the left and the stern on the right, and the canoe wants to turn left after 8 or 10 strokes, what's the easiest way to stop it from turning? Right you are! Switch sides! The bow switches and paddles on the right, and the stern switches and paddles on the left! Simple, yes! Well, no. That's the theory. And it works. That's how the racers paddle long distances at hellishly high speeds. But it's not quite that simple, yet.

The most difficult thing is figuring out when the canoe wants to start that inevitable, inexorable turn to the bow paddler's side, and when to switch side together, on command, one or two strokes before it happens. Most contemporary canoes are designed to hold a reasonably straight course with little effort, because most canoes are used to go somewhere, and a canoe that requires constant attention to make it go straight isn't a pleasant boat for going somewhere, however useful it might be when you're picking your way through a rocky whitewater river. In technical terms, canoes designed for going somewhere (touring canoes) are shaped to provide lateral resistance at their stems. It takes a nudge—and in some cases, the proverbial 2 x 4 you'd use to get a mule's attention—to overcome that lateral resistance. Once the canoe is up and running, it'll go maybe 10 strokes before it wants to turn. Be safe and be successful, though. Switch sides after six strokes.

Here's how to switch. The stern paddler calls the switch, because: (1) the stern paddler is in a better position to feel the stern sliding off course than the bow is, and (2) the stern paddler can see whether or not the bow paddler heard the command and switched, whereas the bow paddler doesn't have that option.

Roberts' Rule 1: Two shalt not paddle on the same side of the canoe, lest the sea rise up and bite them in the butt.

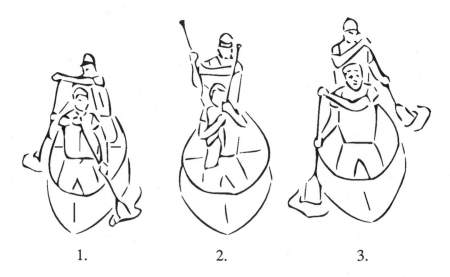

1.   2.   3.

Figure 2-3 Switching sides is as easy as 1-2-3.

Timing counts for something here. Stern paddler, call the switch at the start of a stroke. This gives the bow paddler a chance to get out of the autopilot mode and react to your call, and switch sides at the completion of the stroke. Stern, keep your call a simple monosyllable. "Hut!" is the almost universal call the racers use. It's short, audible, can be grunted, and in the legendary racer and designer Gene Jensen's immortal phrase, "You can say it when you're about ready to throw up." Yes, it does sound silly when you first start doing it. It may even sound intrusive in a paddling situation where quiet is called for. But when you arrive at the point where you can paddle quietly enough to sneak up on a couple of scooter sunning on a log and not disturb them, you'll have a full arsenal of control strokes, and you'll switch for efficiency, not because you must maintain direction. The silly feeling passes quickly. You'll find after fifteen minutes that you can maintain a normal conversation and still say "Hut!" when you need. You hut won't even hear yourhutself saying it afterhut a while, and even if your hut friends think it's nonhutsense, I guarantee that hut you'll get to the takeout hut before they do hut and have first dibs hut on the cold beer hut and cheese and French hut bread you stashed in the hut car.

How To Switch Sides

I'll describe it from the right side. At the completion of the forward stroke, start to remove the paddle from the water as usual. Loosen your right (grip) hand (that's the hand on the paddle shaft, remember?), slide your left (control) hand off the palm grip, and as you lift the paddle out of the water (arms still out in front, just like always), slide your right (grip) hand up the shaft to the handle and "catch" the paddle shaft with your left hand. You can practice this sitting on an armless chair. It takes a few minutes of feeling clumsy, but it's easy to learn. If you really want to feel silly, go outside, with your partner and your paddles, stand in bow/stern alignment, and paddle the air, with the stern calling switches. Sounds dumb. Looks dumb. It works like a charm. It gets you into a "team" mode very quickly. The bow must react to the stern's call, and the stern must respond to the bow's tempo. Dancin', baby! Dancin'!

Remember This?

Now that you know how to switch to maintain direction efficiently without scrubbing off speed with exaggerated correction strokes, you'll be pleased to know that maintaining speed and direction

Figure 2-4 When switching sides (in this case, from right to left) note that the right hand (the former grip hand) is loose, and the thumb isn't wrapped around the paddle shaft. This permits your hand to slide up the shaft and still retain a measure of control.

isn't the real reason for switching sides. It's just one of the reasons. The others? Switching sides lets you equalize the work load on your joints, tendons and muscles; it enables you to make the most powerful, most stable turning strokes, and it gives you a real edge in windy conditions. But more of that later.

Review

As the forward stroke, which I prefer to think of as the "power stroke" because you can use it to provide power in all directions, is fussy to get right, let's break it down again and add a few subtleties while we're at it.

Sit erect but not stiff. Think like a shortstop. Hold the paddle loosely, with your arms extended, but not stiff. Keep your legs out "in front of you" on the footbrace, but not stiff either. I don't want your bony knees sticking up in the air! (As one who once was called "limpet legs" by a singularly handsome young blonde person of the female persuasion, I feel I've paid enough dues to enable me to say that.) Some bow paddlers in narrow fast touring canoes prefer to brace with their knees against the sides of the canoe. This is fine. Whatever keeps your butt firmly in the seat.

The power of the stroke comes from engaging the large muscle groups in your back and shoulders. As you progress, you'll become increasingly aware of starting the stroke from your instep, and you'll feel the power flow from the soles of your feet out to your fingers. To put this power into the paddle blade, you rotate your upper body around the point of the shoulder of your control hand. That's the pivot point, not your waist. If you think waist, you'll over-rotate, off the boat, overpull on the paddle, and waste a lot of energy that should go into keeping the boat moving.

Figure 2-5 Good shoulder rotation here, and an erect, but not stiff body position. Don't drive your shoulder into the stroke until the paddle blade is immersed.

Think of it this way. Sit in a straight chair. Have somebody hold the shoulder of your control hand, not so much to keep it absolutely fixed, but to remind you that it should pretty much stay put and should never (as in King Lear's "Never, never, never, never, never!") move forward. With that hand on your shoulder and your legs relaxed in front of you, reach forward with your grip hand and pretend to grab a stick planted in the bottom of the lake. Don't reach far; if you actually measured how far you extend your grip hand by that rotation, you'd find that it's about five to seven inches, depending on your size. Now, try it with a yardstick. (A paddle's too long for this exercise.) Your arms work together as one unit. You don't push with your control arm and pull with your grip arm. Neither do you cock your control arm for a little extra snap on the stroke. The power comes from the back and shoulders. Think of settling the power into your latissimus dorsi muscles. Feel it? The proper motion is almost up and down, like a piston, rather than forward and back.

Figure 2-6 Whoa, Hoss! This stroke is carried way to far aft! All it's doing is pulling the boat down into the water.

As you get better at this game, you'll find that you tighten up your abdominal muscles a bit with each stroke, and when you really want to make time, you'll straighten up almost imperceptibly as you recover, relax your gut to let a little air sneak in, and tighten down hard in a very brief isometric as you apply power.

You'll notice words like "brief" and "a little" sneaking into this explanation. Here's why. If the tip of your paddle blade travels more than five to seven inches at the point of maximum power, your forward stroke is far too long. Remember, your maximum power is developed when the paddle is within 15 degrees of either side of vertical. Anything more disturbs the progress of the boat. As your paddle takes care of the forward 15 degrees, and your slight rotation around the tip between the time the tip enters the water and the power is applied, you don't need much rotation. What rotation you use should be quick, and the paddle removed from the water as your shoulders come back to square. Unless you're paddling at a frantic tempo, it'll appear from the side that your stroke lingers too long in the water, but that's caused by the fact that the boat is still moving. (Fast, we hope. Effortlessly, we hope.)

Okay, okay. I hear you! You're not a racer! Neither am I any more. Just slow the stroke down a little to where it's more comfortable, and don't "uncoil" as hard, that's all. Keep the stroke light and easy, but use your whole body. Don't paddle sloppily when you're not in a hurry. In fact, greasing through a backwater to sneak up on a raft of Canada geese is the time to learn to paddle with subtle power and elegance.

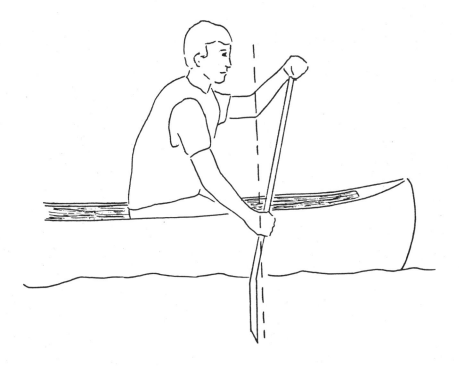

Figure 2-7 This far back and no further!

There's hardly any movement with this stroke. You're still; you're centered over your butt. You're not lunging forward with each stroke to "get more power," because you can't get more power by lunging forward and "punching" your control arm out. Yes, you do drive against the paddle grip, but only when the blade is "set" in the water.

To take the paddle out of the water (the techy term is "recover"), use the same motion in reverse that you did to put the paddle in the water. Up and down; not forward and back. And to backpaddle the canoe, rotate slightly toward the side on which you're paddling, so you start the reverse stroke about where you'd end the forward stroke if you over-rotated a bit, and drive down on the paddle with your grip hand. Again, keep the stroke short. And take note that the bow paddler becomes the stern paddler when the canoe is being backpaddled.

No amount of written instruction can tell you how to control a canoe that's being paddled backward. Try it. Try it and paddle backward for a while just for kicks. Back out of the little duck hole you poked into. Have fun with it, and you'll learn to play the game.

Figure 2-8 The "high recovery" (top) is most efficient, but the "low recovery" (bottom) is very useful when you're bucking a wind, taking your time, or just want look stylish. Let the trailing edge of the paddle blade "kiss" the top of the water as you learn it.

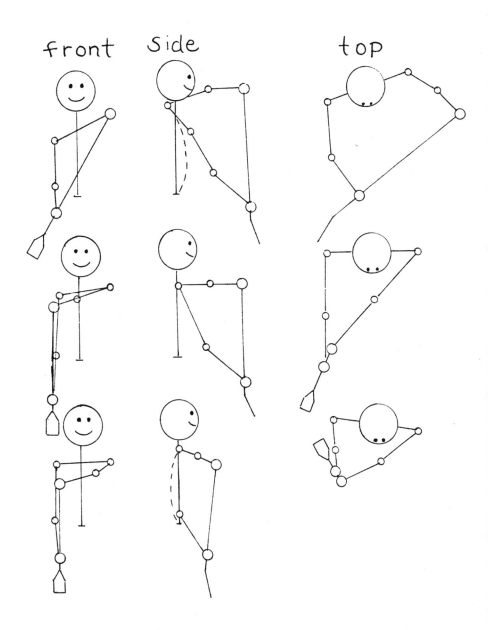

Figure 2-9 A Mechanical Diagram of the Forward Stroke From Top, Side and Front.

3. CORRECTION STROKES

What canoe designer David Yost calls "The Idiot Six"—six power strokes and a switch—works well to maintain direction, but it's about as subtle as a B-52 with 60,000 pound of "dumb bombs" on board. You can add a few refinements to the basic process that will make your paddling more stylish, more quiet and maybe a touch more efficient without putting on the brakes.

For all my talk about the power stroke, the basic forward stroke, the power stroke is only one of the tools in your tool kit. It's the basic tool, no doubt. But you can't build a cathedral with just one tool. So let's open the tool box and poke around inside and see what we find.

The J-Stroke

Ah,hah! Here's our old friend from Camp Yukintipovurtu, the J-stroke! Hmmm. Must have found that at a flea market. Don't toss it in the corner, my friend! Let's get some of the rust off the old J-stroke and put an edge on it, and we'll find it to be a most useful tool.

Remember the diagrams in the old canoeing texts? There's the J, lying flat, and the counselor told you to do it "just like the book says." So you pulled your butt up to the paddle, and pushed out, and performed a short reversing stroke that raised hell with your elbow and just about stopped the canoe in its tracks, but it did keep you on course. Sort of. What you were doing, of course, was compensating for the tendency of the canoe to run to your opposite side after each stroke. And that's what you'll be doing now, but the old, rusty J-stroke is a whole lot sharper, and you don't have to work as hard.

Time was when I wouldn't have used the term "J-stroke," because it was so widely misunderstood. I taught the J-stroke, but I called it a hook stroke. But as I grew older and more respectful of tradition (I'm even rebuilding a 70 year old, Old Town Guide 18), I began calling it the J-stroke again. Besides, the American Canoe Association uses the term, and as an ACA instructor, I'm obliged to use it.

Here's how to do it. Jut before you complete your power stroke, look at the thumb of your control hand (the hand on the grip). If your hand is relaxed, the thumb is either lightly touching the edge of the grip, or, if you paddle with a very open hand as I frequently do, my thumb is pointing almost perpendicular to the keel line of the canoe. It's pointing abeam, if you will. What you need to do to create a small correction in the canoe's course, just enough to almost offset the power stroke, is to give the paddle blade a little twist and flip outward just before the end of the stroke. Relax your control hand. Let the thumb point abeam. And just before you finish your power stroke, twist your control hand counterclockwise if you're paddling on the right side (clockwise if you're on your left side), so that your thumb points

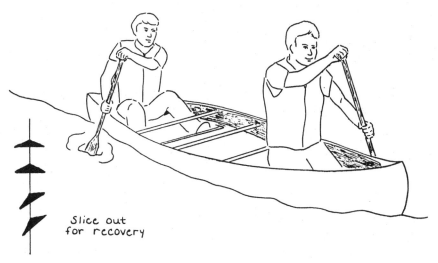

Slice out
for recovery

Figure 3-1 Just a slight twist of the stern paddler's control hand at the point of maximum immersion of the blade is all it takes! Note how small a change in blade angle is necessary.

forward. No, it doesn't have to point at the bow paddler. It needn't be that exaggerated. But it should be quick. And immediately after you point that thumb forward, get the paddle out of the water. Don't let it hang there scrubbing off speed. And don't help the process along by rotating your grip hand. Keep your grip hand loose, and let the paddle shaft rotate within your grip.

Actually, several things happen when you rotate your control hand. The angle of the paddle blade changes, and the resultant of the forces acting on the power face of the blade will push your butt, and therefore the stern of the canoe, over a little to partially compensate for the power stroke. Also, as you can easily find out for yourself if you do the control hand twist slowly, it's nearly impossible to do without dropping your control hand slightly. What actually happens is that your control hand, which is normally at or outboard of the rail of the canoe, moves inboard. So, the paddle blade angle not only alters, but the inboard motion of the grip hand gives the blade a subtle "kick" outward, which pooches the stern back into alignment a bit more. If you're paddling at a fairly quick tempo, say forty strokes per minute or more, you'll be startled to find out who small a correction is necessary to keep the canoe running like an arrow all day. And when you start to work up to the tempo that elite tourers maintain (50-60 light strokes per minute—which is easier to do than to think about), one tiny J-stroke every few strokes and a slight lean to the side opposite will run the boat on rails even in a fairly stiff breeze.

Figure 3-2 The J-Stroke as seen from the rear. Again, there's hardly any change in blade angle. You show your skill by finding the smallest correction necessary to deep the boat tracking, because that's the most efficient correction.

This is a subtle correction. There are times when you may need a more gross correction. (Gross, man!) The answer, of course, is to do the same thing, but start it a bit earlier in the power stroke, and drop your control hand a bit more inboard as you do it. The best way to get a quick sense of how this works is to get the boat up to speed, ask your bow paddler to take his/her paddle out of the water, and play with the correction as the boat continues to glide along. Do this about ten times on both sides, and you'll begin to get a good feel for the correction, and for how little and how much to apply. Your bow paddler will, of course, be bored stiff by this, but not to worry. Once you've figured it out, swap places in the boat and let the bow paddler learn the correction. One of the delights of this style of paddling is that you develop a wonderful versatility. You can paddle bow and stern, and can paddle ambidextrously. This is a far cry from the old days. I can remember one interminable three-day trip when I was saddled with paddling bow for a very large person who could only paddle on the right hand side, and I was nursing a very sore left elbow from a fall in a pick-up basketball game. I would have given my eyeteeth for a stern paddler who could paddle on both sides! In fact, I would have been reasonably content if Lard Butt in the stern paddled at least competently on his right side! But he didn't. Wotthehell; the fishing was good, and I saw my first moose.

In the Bow

Historically, the bow paddler was in charge of the canoe and the stern paddler reacted to the bow. When paddling became more of a recreation than a job, the control sort of sneaked back to the stern. Canoe designer and marketing guru Mike Galt says that this was because women had started paddling with their spouses or boyfriends, and the guys were so caught up in maintaining their macho image that they took over the canoe, and essentially relegated women to a role that more resembled a figurehead than a paddling partner. Mixed-team marathon racers typically put the larger, stronger paddler in the bow, and put the smaller, subtler paddler in the stern, feeling that that's the best way to move the boat, but the responsibility for boat management lies with both paddlers. Sport paddling, a contemporary version of what the Canadians call "style paddling," but done with small, slender, contemporary sport/cruising canoes and bent shaft paddles, returns the control to the bow paddler, and the bow paddler is, by definition, a woman. Galt, who must be credited with this innovative, joyful revival and refinement of a classic way to play in a canoe, should also be credited with returning the control of the boat to the bow in flatwater sport paddling and daytripping. He deserves credit for a lot of other things, too, including knowing how to make Volkswagen vans live forever and being one of the few *gringos* who can make a decent *cafe con leche,* but this isn't the time or place for that essay.

In the touring boat, control lies in the boat itself. Keep the boat happy is the motto. The bow sets the tempo, because the stern can see the bow and pick up on the proper pace. The stern calls the switches, because the stern can check to see that the switch has, in fact, been made. The bow initiates turns, and if need be, the bow calls the switch to set up the turn. The stern is mostly responsible for keeping the boat upright in rough going, because the stern is nearer to the center of buoyancy and has a wider, more stable platform from which to work. But, as either paddler can paddle bow or stern, it doesn't matter in terms of interpersonal relations.

The bow paddler can help maintain direction as needed. In dead-calm water, the stern paddler usually doesn't need any help, and the bow paddler can simply drive the boat hard with a straightforward

Figure 3-3 There's no male or female in a canoe. You're either a paddler or not a paddler. Note, by the way, that both paddle shafts are nearly vertical and that both paddlers have both hands outboard of the rails.

power stroke. Add a touch of wind and/or current, though, and the bow can, by slight adjustment in the direction of the stroke, keep things running smoothly without forcing the stern into gross corrections.

The ideal stroke is parallel to the keel line of the canoe. But a few degrees of variation in this can help keep the boat in line with very little correction in the stern. Let's put the bow on the right and the stern on the left, and let's add a little breeze quartering in from the left. Obviously, if the paddlers switch sides, the stern doesn't have to make much of a correction because the breeze is pushing the bow back in line. But nobody wants to paddle on the same side forever once they've gotten used to switching sides. All the bow has to do is realign the power stroke so it angles ever so slightly into the boat, and bingo!, you're running on rails again, and the stern paddler doesn't have to scrub off speed to make that happen. Teamwork, friends. Teamwork. Keep the boat happy, and you'll be happy.

By the way, I've taken to paddling bow a lot in our big fast touring boat. We have a neat little bow bag that hangs from the carrying thwart and rests on the forward flotation chamber, and it just fits our old 7 x 35 binoculars. It's a whole lot easier for the stern paddler to keep the boat going when the bow stops paddling and vice versa. So, I paddle bow and get to look at birds more. I also get to use my fly rod and some of my ineptly tied flies and poppers. Neat!

Of course, if I play this game to excess, I have been known to receive a wake-up call in the form of a few drops of cold AuSable River water flicked cunningly on the nape of my neck from a very deftly controlled stern paddler.

Figure 3-4 Again – both hands outboard of the rails, but the bow paddler is altering his stroke a bit to drive the bow up into the wind so the stern paddler doesn't bear the brunt of all directional control.

4. TURNING YOUR CANOE

As the editor of the largest paddling publication in the world, I get the opportunity to teach at a lot of public canoe clinics and symposiums. And it's always surprised me to find so many paddlers who are very concerned about how to turn their canoes, because that's actually the easiest part of boat management. The toughest thing to do with a canoe is to make it run straight and true in a wide range of conditions.

Let's look at what it takes to turn a canoe.

Turning By Not Correcting

The easiest way to make a gradual turn is simply to do nothing. You want to turn right? Paddle stern on the left, bow on the right, and neither switch sides nor stick in a J-stroke, and you'll turn to the right. You've just spent a lot of boat time learning how to keep the canoe from following its natural path, which is to turn. Get out of its way and let it turn!

This is fine for big, sweeping bends, and course corrections on a lake. However, it doesn't do much when you need to turn the canoe more quickly. Here's how to do that.

The Draw Stroke

When I'm teaching a class on the water, I hardly ever give a name to a stroke or series of strokes until my class has assimilated most of what they need. Why? If I tell you and show you how to do something, you treat it as a straightforward learning experience and simply do it. If I tell you, "Now we'll learn the draw stroke," you'll start thinking something like, "Oh, oh—my buddy says that this is tough," or "Gosh, I've never been able to do this."

It's tough to disguise names in a book, though. Readers like to have landmarks like chapter headings and subheads to help them find their way through a maze of less-than-deathless prose. Okay. We're talking about the draw stroke. You have thirty seconds to be anxious.

The Static Draw

There are two kinds of draw strokes, static and active. The difference is this. The active draw stroke is, basically, our old friend the power stroke done at an angle of up to 90 degrees with the keel line. There are a few subtleties to it, but it's straightforward. The static draw, which marathon racers and fast touring boat paddlers call a "post" and whitewater kayakers call a "Duffek," in honor of the Czech wizard who developed it, is the simplest stroke you'll ever learn.

Here's how it works. You're in the bow, paddling along at a modest pace. On a whim—bow paddlers can indulge in whims—you stick your paddle blade in the water, shaft vertical and blade parallel to the keel line of the canoe. What happens? You're absolutely right. Nothing happens. Or, more accurately, the small airfoil shape on the backface of

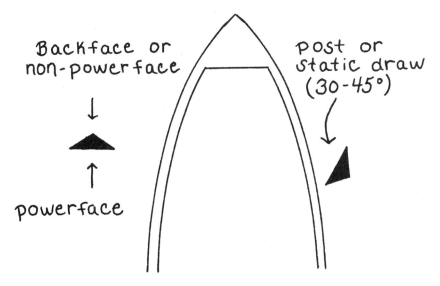

Figure 4-1 Paddle Blade Orientation For the Static Draw Stroke.

the paddle blade doesn't have a large enough effect on the large canoe moving at three knots, and the canoe glides onward. Now, keep the paddle exactly where it is and open the power face of the blade about 30 - 45 degrees to the oncoming water. The backface of the paddle blade will be behind, the power face forward. (There's a piece of tape on the backface, remember?) Now you've created an airfoil that works. You've created an area of negative pressure behind the backface of the paddle blade, and the blade moves into the area. The boat is attached to you; you're attached to the paddle shaft; the shaft's attached to the blade; the blade is moving into the area of low pressure; therefore, the boat moves.

Now, how do your do this when you're not just playing with the paddle? The same way, basically. You're in the bow, on your right. (The stern, of course, is on the left.) Without changing your grip on the paddle, turn your upper body to the right, relax your grip hand so the paddle shaft can turn within it, and with the paddle shaft vertical, open the power face of your paddle 45 degrees to the oncoming water by rotating your control hand clockwise. If you paddle with a relaxed, open hand, the thumb of your control hand (your left thumb), will point at your right shoulder. If the stern paddler simply keeps paddling forward, the canoe will turn to the right. It will turn slowly at first, and faster as the turn progresses.

How can you accelerate the turn? Several ways. You can lean the boat to the side away from the turn. In other words, lean left to turn right; lean right to turn left. There's no magic in this. You could lean right to turn right, but as your paddle shaft is vertical and your paddle blade within 15 degrees of vertical, you don't have much paddle to lean on (to brace against, if you want to get technical). If you lean to the opposite side, you have a brace against the force of the water against the paddle, and the stern paddler is in an excellent position to brace against the lean of the canoe if necessary. It'll feel funny the first few times you do it, but it works, it looks neat, and it feels good.

Another way to accelerate the turn is for the stern paddler to sweep rather than paddle straight ahead. A sweep stroke looks just like you think it would. Instead of rotating your upper body and driving against a vertical paddle shaft and blade that's oriented parallel to the keel line, you sweep the paddle blade out in an arc, which moves the stern of the canoe out while still maintaining way. HINTS: Don't carry the sweep all the way back, because it leaves you in a position from

Figure 4-2 Lean the boat to the opposite side of the turn when you post. This will reduce lateral resistance at both stems and accelerate the turn.

which you can't move into a brace. Also, don't stab at the water or try to thrash the water to a froth. Maintain the same sort of body rotation you use for your power stroke, with your hands away from your body, and maintain a rhythm. You usually can't sweep at the same tempo as you'd maintain for a power stroke, because your paddle blade is in the water over a longer distance. But keep a rhythm and keep smooth, otherwise your bow paddler, who's perched in the narrowest part of the canoe and probably feels somewhat vulnerable, will probably raise a question or two about your ancestry. (There's no question about mine. I sport a bar sinister on my coat of arms—if I had a coat of arms!)

Now that I've introduced the sweep, remember, please, that most paddle strokes can be done in reverse as well as forward. Try the sweep both forward and backward. Try it with the bow sweeping forward and the stern sweeping in reverse, and vice versa. Switch sides and play with the sweep. Get accustomed to powering the stroke with a body rotation rather than with your arms. Go for it! Pick a warm day in shallow water and see how much power you can put into the move. So you get wet! You wanted to take a swim anyway, didn't you?

Let's add another way to accelerate the turn. As the boat swings into the turn, it starts to turn slowly, and then accelerates. Bow paddler, if you sense the swing of the boat and turn your static draw (or post or Duffek) into a power stroke by taking the paddle with you, as it were, with the blade underwater and then kick in your power stroke, the boat will fairly blast out of the turn as the turn is completed.

I know. You're not a racer. You're not interested in going fast. This isn't about going fast. It's about keeping the boat moving once you've got it moving. Any time you let the boat die in the water unintentionally, you have to crank it back up to a constant pace. It's like the difference in gas mileage between city driving and cruising down I-75, only we're talking about miles per gallon of sweat here.

The Active Draw

Sounds like something a busy bartender would do when faced with orders for twelve pitchers of draft, doesn't it? Well, it's something an active paddler does to power the bow of a canoe a few degrees in one direction. And it's not really related to the static draw (post; Duffek) except in the fact that both strokes draw the bow of the canoe toward the paddle. The static draw uses the force of water moving against and past a static paddle blade to "wedge" the bow toward the paddle. The active draw is actually a power stroke, your basic down-and-dirty forward power stroke, done perpendicular to the keel line of the canoe, and many of the same rules apply.

Let's do an active draw. You're paddling bow on your right side. You see something that necessitates a turn to your left. Call the switch. Bow paddlers can do that to take evasive action. Call it loudly, because you're facing forward, and your stern paddler may not hear you if you call the switch softly. Now you're on your left side, and you need to move the bow of the boat to your left. Turn your upper body so you're facing left your shoulders should be almost parallel to the keel line of the canoe. Now, with your arms well away from your body and both hands out over the rail, do a forward stroke. Yep, that's right. A forward stroke done perpendicular to the keel line of the canoe! Right down to all the body rotation you can muster! This will move the bow of the canoe over to the paddle; it will "draw" the canoe to the paddle, which is why it's called a "draw." Of course, by that reasoning, a forward stroke could be called a "draw," too, because it draws the canoe up to the paddle as well. But then...aaah, forget it! This isn't a semantics course.

Okay. Draw the bow of the canoe sideways over to the paddle with a power stroke executed perpendicular to the keel line. No sweat, so far. But a problem is about to arise. Your paddle blade is in the water, and the canoe is moving toward it. If you don't do something with the paddle blade, the canoe will run over it, and before you're able to let go of the paddle, you'll be pole-vaulted over the rail and into the water and your stern paddler will be much amused. You won't tip the canoe. You'll just be launched, and the canoe will continue on its merry way.

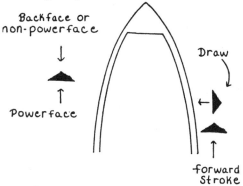

Figure 4-3 Paddle Blade Orientation For the Active Draw Stroke.

There are two ways to avoid being a Scud missile with a PFD. The easiest way is to simply rotate up and pick the paddle out of the water, and make another draw stroke. This works, but it rocks the boat, literally, and it looks ugly. No point lookin' ugly when you can look good, so instead of lifting the paddle from the water, keep it in the water and an underwater recovery into another draw. Here's how.

At the completion of the draw (you're paddling on the left, remember), point the thumb of your control hand (your right hand) away from the boat, as close to 90 degrees as you can manage, and

Figure 4-4 Don't be afraid to get some body rotation into the active draw stroke. It's a stroke you'll use when the boat must be moved right now, so learn to do it with power.

push the paddle, with its blade feathered perpendicular to the keel lin of the canoe, back out again with your grip arm and shoulder. Rotate your control hand back to the power stroke position, and draw again. HINTS: Your control hand hardly moves at all in a draw. It's well outboard of the rail, and essentially stays there in one spot in space and time while you provide the power for the draw by rotating with the shoulder of your grip arm. The active draw is a power move; if you don't need to move the bow over right now, don't waste your energy. Use a static draw. Will you do it right the first time? No. This isn't an easy stroke to learn. No stroke is. Practice it, and crank up the power as you feel better about your progress.

You've looked at how to make the canoe go straight and how to turn the boat with static and active draw strokes from the bow. You can go straight—no mean accomplishment in these perilous times—and you can turn left and right. Let's review some of the elements of good turning strokes before we move on. And we will be moving on. There are a few more things you should have in your tool kit before you take that once-in-a-lifetime trip.

Putting The Strokes Into Practice

The mechanics of the static and active draw strokes are pretty straightforward. Yes; they'll take you some time to perfect, but there are a few games you can play to hasten the learning process, and make the strokes so much a part of your body's response that you don't have to think of how to do them when you need to do them.

Lakeshore Slalom

One of the most pleasant ways to develop boat-handling skills is to paddle the perimeter of a lake, and simply view every dock, every swimming float, every moored boat, every lilly pad and every overhanging branch as an obstacle to be avoided. As you get better and better at this game, try to miss the object by as little as possible. Start with the lilly pads; they're a lot softer than rocks and docks while you learn and build your confidence. In a short time, you'll find yourself fairly screaming up to an obstruction and snapping the boat around it without scrubbing off hardly any speed at all.

Doughnuts

This is a fun game you can use for learning the active draw and for a short warm-up when you first put your boat in the water. It stretches the muscles of your upper torso, and it helps you "feel" the boat.

It's simple enough. The bow paddler draws on one side, and the stern paddler draws on the other side. If your boat is trimmed right, and you're feeling what each other is doing, the boat should pivot in circles around its midpoint. Cut some doughnuts in one direction, call a switch, and cut a few in the other direction. Stop and regroup when you start giggling uncontrollably.

Switch Positions

If your weights are such that you can trim the canoe level if you swap paddling positions, take every opportunity you can to do so. Cut some doughnuts; paddle a lakeshore slalom; go have fun. Remember, if you paddle this way you must be able to paddle bow and stern, and be comfortable working from both sides of the boat. Be patient. If you've paddled stern all your life, you'll probably be flummoxed by paddling bow with a newcomer to the task of paddling stern. This is particularly true with husband/wife teams. Be supportive of each other's efforts, please. Be patient, please. You didn't learn to paddle your regular position in a day. Molly and I will switch positions in the boat regularly—sometimes three or four times in a single day of paddling. It keeps us fresh, it gives us a different perspective, it lets us use slightly different muscle groups, and it gives us the flexibility to jump in the right seat at the right time to better serve the boat. It also enables us to paddle with anybody who paddles this style. Any time, any river, any paddler.

River Strategy

As we've mentioned, as you've also figured out, this style of paddling requires the bow paddler to be on the side to which the canoe is to be turned, and the stern paddler on the opposite side. There's a good reason for this. An onside turning stroke is more powerful, more easily controlled more easily turned into a forward stroke, and more stable than the cross-body draw stroke (crossdraw or crossover). It also maintains the stern paddler in the right position for a bracing move or for other moves to deal with river obstacles.

Visualize this. You're making a right turn on a river that's moving along pleasantly. As you make the turn, bow on the right and stern on the left, with the canoe leaned slightly to the left (the downstream side), the river flow is constricted by a jumble of logs piled up by high water on the left bank. The increased current swings the stern of the canoe toward the logs. No problem. The stern paddler can put in a strong reverse sweep, which will push the stern away from the logs, and the bow paddler can power the hull out of trouble. If you're paddling bow left and stern right, and paddling with the classic technique that doesn't permit switching sides, and entering each turn with the bow on the side to which the boat is being turned, the bow paddler sets up the turn with a cross-body draw and the stern paddler uses an exaggerateed correction stroke (probably a very deep J-stroke). As the current grabs the stern of the canoe and sweeps it toward the logs on river left, the stern paddler's only recourse is to draw the stern of the canoe up into the current. Drawing upstream is tricky business. The stroke isn't as effective, because the flow of water is coming at you, and the current may well wedge your paddle under the canoe faster than you can say Ruby Tuesday.

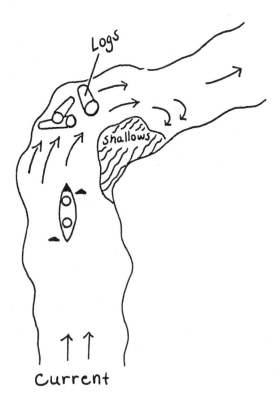

Figure 4-5 With the bow paddler on the right and the stern on the left, it's a lot easier to keep the boat away from the logs. "Classic" technique might require that the bow paddler perform a cross-body maneuver, which leaves both paddlers on the same side of the boat and in a less stable position.

Let's make the situation simpler. You're swinging through a right turn in calm water with just a hint of current, and you're paddling properly, with the bow paddler on the right and the stern on the left. As the canoe swings around the turn, it hits a submerged log that you couldn't see because the water was murky and there wasn't enough current to produce a tell-tale ripple downstream. It's a good, solid bump; the canoe stops in its tracks for a moment before it slides over the log. As it stops, both paddlers are moved sharply against the left rail of the canoe, but the stern paddler has the presence of mind to drop into a low brace just before the canoe rolls. It's not a difficult move, because the stern paddler is on the left side already, and probably sweeping to help the bow paddler make the turn. If you're a traditional paddler, with the stern on the right and the bow on the left, the bow paddler has probably done a cross-bow draw to initiate the turn, and when the boat hits the log, both paddlers are on the right, or upstream, side and the canoe is rolling over to the left. What to do? Drop back five and punt. It's about all you can do, unless you're very, very well schooled.

Initiation

Once you've learned your turning strokes and feel pretty comfortable with them, you'll find yourself paddling with an experienced team of paddlers one day, and you'll be amazed at how easily they slide their long, fast touring canoe around obstructions. You're doing well, not to worry. But you know that their boat is harder to turn than yours. It's longer and leaner and it doesn't have as much rocker, and they're aggressive with that boat. They just flat-out scream into turns—and make the whole thing look so easy. How can you do that?

They're initiating their turns with a set-up stroke that makes their turning strokes that much more efficient. Let's set up for a right turn. You know the drill: bow on the right, stern on the left. You stick in a post or a draw, and you turn. They stick in a post or a draw, and the boat fairly snaps around. They could have done several things to initiate the turn and make it more effective. The obvious stroke is a stern sweep done before the bow puts in the draw. More likely, the stern sweeps and the last forward stroke the bow puts in before planting the draw is a forward done maybe 30 degrees off the line parallel to the keel. It's generally called a "quarter draw," although it can be at any angle short of 90 degrees to the keel line. This quartering power stroke (or draw stroke—it does a bit of both) does two things. Obviously, it sets up the turn while still maintaining momentum into the turn. And it does one subtle little thing that you'd never notice unless you paddle solo canoes, especially solo whitewater canoes, which react very quickly to the paddle. If you're sitting in the bow and you turn your torso 90 degrees to the right to plant a draw (or even 45 degrees), the act of turning your torso to the right will kick the bow of the canoe a bit to the left if the boat is highly responsive, or scrub off some of the effect of the stern paddler's sweep if the boat is a directionaly stable tourer. It isn't much, but it does affect the boat. Initiating the turn with the quarter draw in the bow and the sweep in the stern overcomes this. What does it translate to in terms of energy saving? A good bit, if the river is twisty. It means that you go into the turn faster, carry your speed through the turn, and come out faster, and you've taken four or five fewer strokes in the process. This adds up to a lot more miles per gallon of sweat in the course of a day.

In the same vein, don't switch and go immediately into a draw if you can help it. Make the switch two strokes earlier, and let the stern initiate that right turn with a hard, deep correction stroke on the right before he or she switches to the left and drops into a sweep.

When you've gotten comfortable with these little tricksy bits that save your energy and get you down the river or across the lake looking like a pro, we'll show you how to take advantage of moving water in such a way that only the very best paddlers will be able to spot the exact strokes you used to turn your canoe. But that's for later.

For now, go take a run at that dock on the lake, initiate your turn a stroke or two before, and carve a turn around the end of it that will have the folks on the front porch of their cottage standing up and cheering!

A touch of the bill of your cap and a short salute is the proper acknowledgement. To ignore applause shows no class.

5. GOING SIDEWAYS

Huh? C'mon Uncle Harry! You've been telling me how hard it is to learn to paddle forward, and now you want me to paddle sideways? Are you sure that's just Gevalia Traditional Roast in your coffee cup?

Believe it. It's just coffee. And you need to know how to make your canoe go sideways. The fancy name is "sideslip", and it's necessary in moving water. In still water, it won't save your boat, but it can save a lot of efforts.

Here's the situation. You're paddling the classic Adirondack Canoe route from Old Forge to the Saranacs (or to Tupper Lake, which is how I always preferred to end it). You've carried from Raquette Lake (it was windy, wasn't it?) into Forked Lake, and you've ridden a crisp westerly down the lake to the shallow, rocky outlet so you can register for a campsite with the ranger. You're zipping along at a good clip, and there's a large granite boulder a few boat lengths dead ahead, and four inches under the water. The water's gin-clear, but the waves were busy enough that you didn't notice it. What do you do?

You can backpaddle, and you'll probably stop in time to avoid the ego-deadening "thunk" that says "You blew it!" to the whole universe. But, with a loaded canoe, a good head of steam, and riding a following wind, you might not stop in time. You could turn, but the wind and waves might slow the turn enough for the stern to slide into or onto the rock. Help!

Help is on its way. Bow paddler, stick in a draw, a hard draw. Stern paddler, your bow paddler has just put in a hard draw, and you don't know why, TRUST YOUR BOW PADDLER. Your bow paddler wouldn't do that out of a clear blue sky. There must be something up there that imperils the canoe. Don't think. Don't analyze. Push the stern of the canoe away from your paddle so that the canoe is moving forward and sideways, bow and stern still aligned. If your bow puts in another draw, just keep pushing the stern away from the paddle, and keep doing it until the bow drops back into a forward stroke.

Whew! that was close! You missed the boulder—and the canoe's still zipping along with very little loss of speed. Now's the time to backpaddle. It gets quite rocky here, and you'll have to pick your way through to the takeout at the ranger station.

Now let's look at just what you did as a team. The bow paddle moved the boat sideways with an active draw stroke. If there had been a boat length more warning, the bow may simply have chosen a static draw (or a post). The stern did the reverse of an active draw, a stroke called a pushaway. You know how to do a draw in the stern. Instead of starting the draw well away from the canoe, with your torso nearly parallel to the keel line, you start the pushaway with the paddle close to the boat, the blade fully submerged, and apply the power by rotating your upper body and directing the thrust away from the canoe. Feather the paddle blade just like you did with the draw, except now you're returning the blade to the boat feathered rather than moving it away from the boat feathered, and do it again if you need to. One pushaway in the stern for each draw in the bow is the rule of thumb, and please try to do the strokes together. Stern, watch your bow! TRUST YOUR BOW.

An Aside

Guys, if you're paddling with your wife or that special friend in the bow, here's the instance that shows whether you're a paddler or Captain Macho. If you miss the rock, you both did your job. If you hit the rock, you both blew it. There is room in a canoe for a lot of things. Pierre Berton once observed that a Canadian is somebody who can make love in a canoe, and the irrepressible Philip Chester capped Mr. Berton's observation by noting that you had to know how to remove

Figure 5-1 Face your work when you do any stroke. It requires a bit of flexibility to face your work when you do a pushaway, but your power comes from facing your work.

the center thwart. Room enough indeed! But there is *never* room enough in a canoe for placing blame. There's room for figuring out what went wrong, and there's room for learning, but there's *never* room in a canoe for placing blame. Not in our canoe, and not in your canoe if you want to paddle with us.

We'll cover the pushaway again when we talk more about moving water. Just remember that moving water does bizarre things to canoes when they get crosswise to the current, and work on your pushaway. It's not an easy stroke to learn. It goes against all your common sense to move strongly away from the boat. Until you have the stroke down solidly, remember that a reverse sweep will also push the canoe away from the paddle. The drawback to the reverse sweep is that it slows the canoe down more than the pushaway. If you come from a whitewater tradition or a classic tradition, you could use a "pry stroke." I've used countless prys in the stern of my short class downriver racing canoe, but I prefer the pushaway for touring paddlers using bent shaft paddles in still water, moving water and touring whitewater, and I don't teach the pry to them. And I'm not going to teach it here.

Why the pushaway? A couple of reasons. It's smoother than the pry—and there are times when smooth is important. It leaves you in a position to move directly into another stroke, be it another pushaway, a brace or a forward stroke. And because the power phase of the pushaway is about the same length as the power phase of the draw the bow paddler's using, the boat doesn't wiggle and jiggle. It feels stable at a point when you may very well need that feeling of stability. Let's look at the mechanics of the pushaway one more time. It's not an easy stroke to learn, because you're doing some things that run counter to your common sense.

Fine Points And Fussiness

All strokes have many elements in common. If you think of the pushaway as a reverse power stroke done 90 degrees to the keel line of the canoe, you won't go wrong.

1. Start the stroke just like you'd finish a draw.
2. Maintain the same placement of your grip hand as you do for all other strokes—about 2 1/2 hand widths up the shaft from the blade.
3. Face your work.
4. Keep the paddle shaft vertical and both hands outboard of the rails.
5. As you rotate the shoulder of your grip hand outward, remember that you're pivoting around the point of your control hand's shoulder.
6. Your control hand hardly moves at all.
7. The entire stroke is no "longer" than a draw. We know that the maximum force of any stroke is exerted for only seven inches or so; the boat's momentum moves it further than that distance. You don't have to hang your upper body out over the rail!
8. If you drop the shoulder of your grip hand as you rotate, your head—and your entire center of gravity—will lower,—and the canoe will remain stable.

And remember this. Practice produces perfection if you practice perfectly, and perfect practice produces pleasurable paddling. (Wow! I've always wanted to say that!)

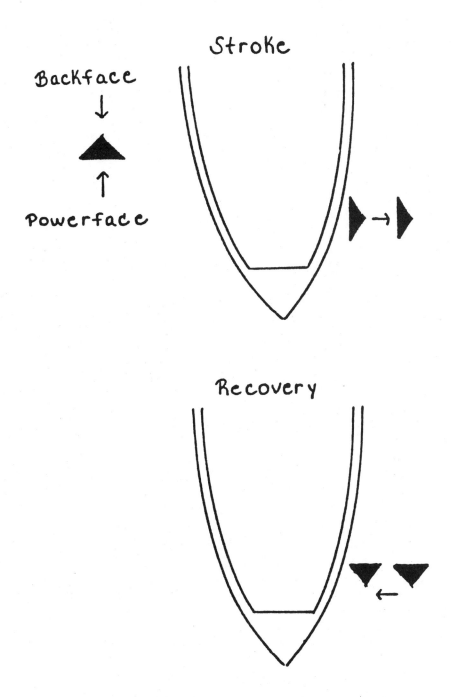

Figure 5-2 Schematic of Paddle Blade Positions for the Pushaway.

6. KEEPING THE WATER OUT

When you get right down to it, Steve Scarborough is right. There aren't many things you have to do with a canoe. You have to make it go forward and backward, turn it right and left, move it sideways, and keep the river it its proper place, which is outside and beneath the canoe. In a fair and just world, if you can make the canoe go forward and back, turn right and left, and move sideways, you've accomplished 98 percent of what you have to do to keep the river in its place. Let me bore you with a story.

Back when Molly and I ran two outdoor shops and a cross—country ski area, we taught paddling a lot, both kayaking and canoeing. In winter, the introductory kayaking classes were conducted in a swimming pool, because Upstate New York water is frequently stiff in January and February. It took what could euphemistically be called "force of character" to keep the novice kayakers on track. They'd all come from a canoeing background, and were incensed by the idea that we wanted them to learn to control their boats before we started teaching them to roll up. They finally got the idea that good paddling skills and sound mechanics would enable them to control their boats in such a way that they might not have to roll up as often. Bingo!

I'll show you two strokes that will keep the river in its place. Just remember that the better you manage all the other strokes, the less likely you'll be to need these.

42

The Low Brace

The basic "Ohmigod!" stroke for canoeists and kayakers alike is the "low brace." The common image of the stroke is one of a paddler falling on his paddle with a resounding slap that sounds like a beaver on steroids. The proper image to fix in your mind is a quick, subtle move that's mostly done by body position, and that flows directly into a stroke.

It's easier to learn a low brace in a solo canoe, or in a tandem canoe paddled solo from amidships. This doesn't mean that you can't learn it in a tandem canoe; you just have to maintain good rapport with your partner.

Here's how it works. Hold the paddle as if you were taking a forward stroke, then place it horizontal, the knuckles of your control hand down, the back face of the blade flat to the water, away from the canoe and out beside your hips. Your control hand should be about at your belly button, your body comfortably erect and elbows bent

Figure 6-1 Try to keep both hands outside of the boat for the most effective low brace. Note how much reach you gain and how much lower your head and body are in the upper illustration than in the lower one. Learn this stroke kneeling, and then learn it from a sitting position. It'll be easier that way.

slightly. Now lean on the paddle and push down into the water. Start with a slight lean, and increase it as you feel comfortable. Recover by lifting you control hand. Why? If you push down against the water with your grip hand, you weight will be too far outboard for the small paddle blade to support you. The blade will sink, with you attached to it. Lift your control hand. This moves your body against the roll of the boat, and rights it. The paddle does very little beyond giving you a moment's purchase against which to move your body. Once you have the mechanics of which hand to move under control, do it some more, but this time, drop your head and shoulders to lower your roll center. Works better, eh? No surprise. You shortened the lever arm that wants to roll you over.

Let's get braver. Let your control hand move further and further outboard as you practice, until both hands are outboard of the canoe's rails. Try to get the knuckles of you control hand wet, and then the wrist. Drop your head and shoulders down inside the rails. Great! Your canoe was tipped far enough over to take in water, and you braced back up smoothly!

But, sooner or later, you didn't make it. You needed one more brace, but the paddle sank out of sight before you could do it—and took you with it. For a simple low brace, with your control hand inboard at about your belly button, recovering the paddle is easy. For those times when the going is tough, you must get the paddle back to the surface so you can either brace again or move directly into an active stroke. As you lift your control hand, turn it so your thumb is pointing upward at about 30 degrees, and rotate your upper body slightly. This will drive the paddle in what looks and feels like a very short, powerful reverse sweep with the power directed downward. The blade will climb to the surface, and you're ready to brace again or move the canoe forward or sideways.

This is fine—so far. Either paddler can and must be able to brace from either side of the boat and from either bow or stern. It's obvious that the stern paddler is in a position to execute a more powerful brace than the bow, but the boat doesn't always roll to stern paddler's side! What do you do if you're the offside paddler? The simplest thing you can do is to drop your head and shoulders to lower the roll center of the boat, and brace on your side. This gets your weight low and over the offside rail, and your paddle ready to catch the boat when it rolls back

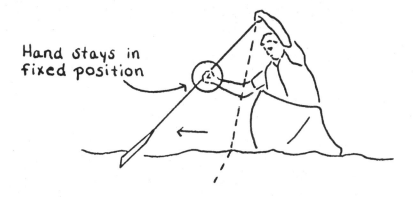

Hand stays in fixed position

Figure 6-2 The Dynamic High Brace. It's really a pry stroke (a hard pushaway with your grip hand essentially "fixed" as a pivot) dome from an Omigod position. Play with this on a warm summer's day on (and it!) a warm lake.

up. There's also a quick levering stroke that looks like nothing so much as a badly placed pry that will help you recover from an offside roll. I've diagrammed it for you, and I can tell you that it works and that you'll learn it only by seeing it done and trying it. It requires instantaneous response; if you're late, and put it in when your partner has started to brace the boat back up, you can easily cause an upset to your side. Play with this some warm day on a warm lake with a sandy bottom. And if you're really hard-core about it, have a friend stand waist-deep in the water at the stern of your canoe and provide some unpredictable wave action for you. You need a solid brace most of all when you're not expecting it!

The High Brace

This is a classic maneuver. It's pretty, graceful, effective, and can be easily turned into a draw or a forward stroke. Most paddlers think of it as a bow stroke, but it works in the bow or the stern

The "high brace" looks almost like our old friend the static draw stroke (or Duffek), with a couple of differences. Draws, either static or active, are done with your upper torso rotated so you can face your work, as it were. You don't always have the time to do that when you need a brace. And the paddle shaft is vertical or nearly so when you draw, because a draw is really a power stroke put in 90 degrees to the keel line of the canoe. The high brace is usually done with the shaft angle nearer 45 degrees to the water than 90 degrees,and the direction of the power stroke is down and toward the boat rather than toward the boat alone. The active part of the brace, the part of the brace in which you're exerting force on the paddle blade, is very short. The high brace is a favorite of sea kayakers and whitewater kayakers, because it's really a part of the Eskimo roll. You could make a case for the roll as nothing more that a high brace from a very awkward position. At any rate, you can tip a kayak to 90 degrees and the river won't come in. You can't do that with an open boat. The best application of the high brace in the open boat is to impart a short-term steadying factor as you look for the right time to power out, turn or sideslip. It's a particularly comfortable stroke for the bow paddler, because the bow paddler must always be prepared to apply power or set up a turn, and it's always easier to do from a firm platform.

To Avoid Confusion

If you take a paddling course from an instructor certified by the American Canoe Association (ACA), the high brace will be called a static draw or a Duffek. That quick little pry to lever your boat back up when you're being rolled to your off side is called a high brace. This isn't a new term; neither is it a new stroke. But both the term and the stroke have been used primarily in open boat whitewater instruction, and haven't penetrated public consciousness with respect to open canoe touring skill development. The change in nomenclature is logical, and promotes a greater accuracy in talking about stroke mechanics. As an ACA instructor, I confess that I should have used ACA terminology throughout. In this case, I didn't. I chose to go with terms that would be more familiar to you, and clear up the nomenclature change after you'd learned the strokes.

Practice, Practice, Practice!

Go from a hanging draw to a draw to a forward power stroke to a low brace. Vary the sequence. You should, in time, be able to go from any stroke to any other stroke—which may well include switching sides—with absolute ease, and without thinking about it. Remember: the only stroke you'll ever take that isn't part of a sequence is the last one you take when you come to shore.

7. IN WIND AND WAVE

It always struck me as strange that all canoeing books spend countless pages telling you how to paddle moving water and whitewater, yet ignoring how to paddle in wind and waves. The skills are related, in the sense that good stroke mechanics, a calm demeanor, bone-deep teamwork and a boat suited to the environment are essential. So, what makes paddling in wind and waves different? Several things. To begin with—and maybe even to end with—there aren't any eddys on a big, windswept bay. You can't pop behind a rock in the current and find a little patch of calm in which to take a deep breath and make a plan for approaching what lies downstream. If you blow it, there's a long, long swim in store. It may not be as violent a swim as a heavy rapid can give you, but rapids end in pools, sooner or later. Lakes end at the shoreline—and a half-mile swim in the 42 degree water of Lake Superior into the teeth of a wind is serious business. Finally, wind waves move; river waves are generally stationary. Lakes stay still; lake waves move. Rivers move; river waves stand still.

There's one rule governing all big water paddling. Write it indelibly on the back of your hand; chisel it into your memory. *If it's bad now, it will probably get worse.* Stay on shore or get to shore and wait it out. Yes, there are exceptions to this. You'll learn those exceptions as you grow in skill, experience and wisdom. But I grew up on a big lake. I live 1/2 mile by river from a very big lake, Lake Huron. I've spent a lot of time paddling in the Gulf of Mexico and other such bodies of water. And my partner, Molly, is as good a wind and wave paddler as you'll find anywhere. And we always have a couple of books and the binoculars and bird guide with us for those days when we say, "No way!" Maybe we could have paddled. If we were in an emergency situation, like one of the party having had a heart attack, we would have paddled, and made it. But we paddle for pleasure. And while it's fun to push the envelope sometimes—if the water's warm and the boat is empty—four hours of living on the edge in a survival situation isn't what most folks are seeking.

Paddling Upwind

Most paddlers get worried at the thought of running upwind, bucking the waves in which to work. You can see the waves coming, and you can paddle actively rather than reactively.

If the waves aren't high, the simplest strategy is to run right up the gut and deal with them head-on. This puts a lot of spray in your bow paddler's face, and the boat loses speed because it's pitching up and down as much as it's going forward, but it has the charm of simplicity. The artist's way is to take the waves at an angle when they're high and run up into them at each momentary lull. Waves are never uniform. They'll come in sets of big ones and smaller ones, and sometimes you can find a relatively "flat" section that you can just hammer through.

Quartering up into waves is a little more wiggly than running them head-on. The orbital motion of the water particles in the crest of a wave are moving against the canoe at the time when the bow is most fully buried, and the canoe is moved off a level orientation by the slope of the wave face. You've added another component of motion, roll, to the pitch component you deal with running straight upwind.

When running straight upwind, switch sides frequently to flush the fatigue products from your muscles. You're working hard when you paddle upwind. do what you can to ease the fatigue. As you grow more skilled, and start attacking waves at angles when the opportunity presents itself, keep the stern on the downwind side of the canoe and the bow upwind. This puts the bow in the position to draw up into the wind and waves as needed, and keeps the stern in the position to naturally drive the bow of the boat into the wind to keep it from turning sideways and wallowing in the trough of the wave (broaching).

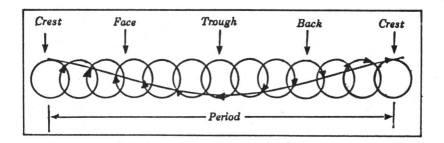

Figure 7-1 The Anatomy of a Wave. Water particles are moving in a circular fashion within a wave, and this affects your boat.

Paddling Downwind.

Looks like fun, eh? You've just left the dock at Clearwater Lodge in Minnesota's Boundary Waters Canoe Area, fueled with anticipation and clearwater's pancakes. You dawdled over coffee (you always dawdle over coffee at Clearwater Lodge!), and the prevailing westerlies are already dappling the big lake with catspaws, even at the lee shore. Wow! This is going to be an easy ride down to the 214 rod portage into West Pike!

Well maybe not. Paddling a following sea with comfort and aplomb is one of the high points of the art. What should be a piece of cake can be turned into a horror show. A canoe running down the face of a wave gains speed rapidly, propelled by wind, wave and the orbital flow of the wave itself. And when the canoe hits the trough of the wave, the bow buries, the canoe starts to run uphill, the orbital motion of the wave restrains its passage, and the stern "half" of the canoe is still accelerating. You're about to become a submarine—unless you're paddling a little off the wind. Then, the stern will swing crosswise as it slides down the face of the wave. Oh, my, Maynard, you told me this would be easy! What are we going to do? First, relax. If you're stiff, your head and shoulders are so much dead weight at the end of a three-foot lever arm that does nothing but raise the roll center of the canoe at a time when you least want a high roll center. Let the canoe roll under you as you paddle, using you hips and footbraces to effect control while your upper body rolls loosely and stays centered over your hips.

You can roll a canoe right up to the rail with no consequences if your nose is over your hips and relaxed. Stiffen up, and you're swimming for sure! Enjoy the sleigh ride. Revel in it, and in your control of the situation. Paddle with the calm of a Zen archer shooting out the flame of a candle. Feel the waves act on the canoe. Roll with them.

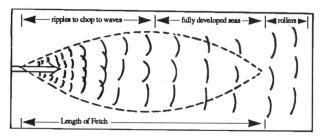

Figure 7-2 Wave Propagation
It may be calm when you start running downwind, but when you get to the other end of the lake, watch it!

Strategies? in a following sea, the bow maintains way, the stern maintains direction. Switches are always called by the stern paddler—and don't expect many. If the waves are quartering in on the right, the stern will be on the left side, because a pushaway or a reverse sweep will keep the canoe from sliding down the face of the wave and broaching in the trough. This also puts the stern on the appropriate side for a brace. Keep the canoe from accelerating (surging) down the face of a wave, keep it from stalling in the trough of the wave, and keep it from spinning on top of the wave as the wave bears under its middle and you'll do just fine. Don't just drift through following seas, though. If you're moving at wave speed, you're at the mercy of the waves. Be more aggressive as your skills improve. Too much enthusiasm may sometimes get you into trouble, but too little enthusiasm will always get you into trouble.

Paddling In Beam Seas

Paddling across the waves requires the greatest degree of "feel" of all big water paddling modes, because there's more happening to the canoe in a beam sea.

Objects in the water tend to make the same motion as the water they displace. A canoe in a beam sea will follow the same circular motion as the orbiting particles in the wave that moves beneath it. There's not much relative motion between the canoe and the water. It's not always comfortable, but it's safe. But, add paddlers to the canoe,

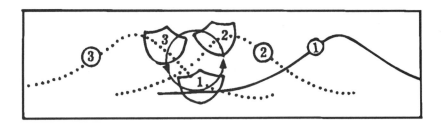

Figure 7-3 The Movement of a Canoe in a Beam Sea

and the roll center is well above the waterline. This isn't a problem either, if you stay relaxed and fluid as the wave slips underneath. If you can't, the slight angle that the canoe assumes—leaning leeward on the wave face, leaning windward on the back of the wave, and passing through a neutral point at the crest and in the trough—will be magnified. Remember this: the canoe will easily change from a leeward lean to a windward lean before the relatively high and heavy mass of your body will.

Physical law plays a big part here. It doesn't take a huge sea to wreak havoc. One of the two "worst" seas to take abeam is a sea whose crests are twice the canoe's beam at the load waterline apart. Why? The wave period is so short that the canoe is either rolling leeward or windward, or passing through the neutral zone so quickly that the rate of roll becomes difficult to adjust to. And that's not a spectacular sea! In fact, the average 17-18 footer, with a beam at the load waterline of 34 inches, hits that kind of complication in a wave height of about 10 inches in deep water, because a 10-inch wave in deep water will have a period (length from crest to crest) of about 68 inches.

The other "worst wave" to take abeam is a breaking wave, because the breaking wave violates the predictable orbital motion. The canoe starts to rise on the wave face and leans to leeward, and then gets hammered by water falling from the crest of the wave at the point of maximum lean! It doesn't take a lot of imagination to figure out what happens next!

How to paddle in a beam sea? Stay loose. I know; you've heard that before. I meant it then, and I mean it now. Enjoy, enjoy, enjoy. Keep the stern paddler on the leeward side, the bow on the windward.

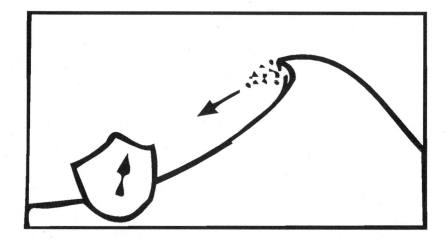

Figure 7-4 Breaking Wave and Beam Sea Normally, you brace into a wave. But if you brace into a breaking wave with an open boat, you'll fill up with water. You may well have to lean away from the wave and drop into a low brace in the stern and a brace in the bow.

This keeps the effective brace where it needs to be, and also positions the bow paddler for the option to draw up into and over the wave crest and run for a set of smaller waves. In big waves, it's sometimes useful to lean the canoe a bit to the lee side. This is a bit like weighting the downhill ski; your senses rebel against the notion. But it's a way to keep big waves and breaking waves from dropping into the canoe. Stay alert. Nasty, steep short-period waves can be run by quartering into them as you head for the bigger but longer-period stuff to run in the trough. It may seem more intimidating, but it's a smoother ride.

Hints

Dave Getchell Sr., a wonderfully sensible man, once offered us some wonderfully sensible advice. If the wind is kicking up to where paddling is a problem, and there's a shoreline that permits it, tow the canoe along the shore! It never occurred to me, so help me! I've had occasion to use that advice since, and it works. Also, if you have to round a narrow point, and the waves look like killers off the point, head for shore and see if you can portage across the point and put in on sheltered water.

Games For The Windbound

Canoe designer John Winters suggests that you wow your friends by calculating the speed of waves for them. Multiply the time it takes for two wave crests to pass a fixed point (a floating stick is just fine) by 5.6, and you'll get the wave speed in kilometers per hour. Now that beats the heck out of bragging about how many stitches per inch are in the shoulder seams of your anorak! And if you're really stuck for amusement, and have already exhausted simple Zen stuff like "Why did the First Patriarch come from the west?", start on the 39 Articles of Religion in the Book of Common Prayer of the Episcopal Church.

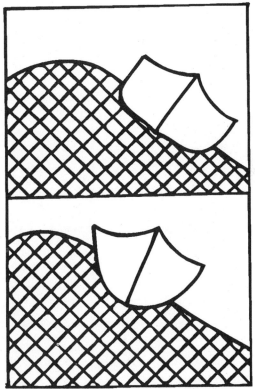

Figure 7-5 A canoe with a flat bottom reacts more quickly in a beam sea, and follows the contour of the wave, which can put it in a very unstable condition. The rounder hull has less freeboard, but reacts more slowly, and rides out the wave in a more upright attitude.

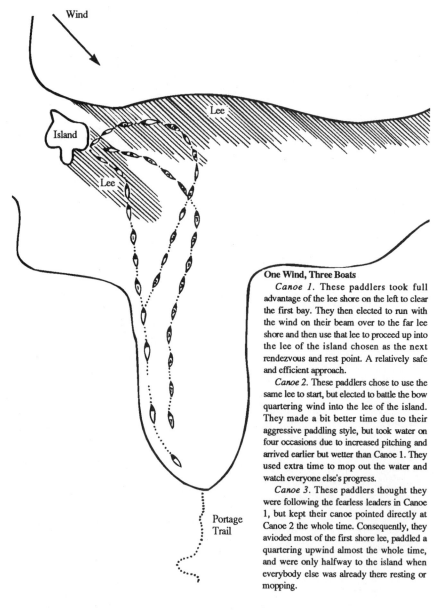

One Wind, Three Boats

Canoe 1. These paddlers took full advantage of the lee shore on the left to clear the first bay. They then elected to run with the wind on their beam over to the far lee shore and then use that lee to proceed up into the lee of the island chosen as the next rendezvous and rest point. A relatively safe and efficient approach.

Canoe 2. These paddlers chose to use the same lee to start, but elected to battle the bow quartering wind into the lee of the island. They made a bit better time due to their aggressive paddling style, but took water on four occasions due to increased pitching and arrived earlier but wetter than Canoe 1. They used extra time to mop out the water and watch everyone else's progress.

Canoe 3. These paddlers thought they were following the fearless leaders in Canoe 1, but kept their canoe pointed directly at Canoe 2 the whole time. Consequently, they avioded most of the first shore lee, paddled a quartering upwind almost the whole time, and were only halfway to the island when everybody else was already there resting or mopping.

Figure. 7-6:   Strategy For Lake Crossing in Wind.

8. IN MOVING WATER

There are some things you should know about paddling techniques as they apply to moving water. This isn't a book about whitewater; neither is it a book about river reading. It's a book about paddling technique. But some strokes and combinations of strokes apply directly to moving water, and you should know what they are and how to use them

The Cross Ferry

The cross ferry makes use of the current to enable you to zip across a river easily whether you're going either upstream or downstream. The downstream cross ferry is more commonly know as a "backferry," because you're really using reversing strokes to hang the boat in the current. Let's start with the backferry, because it's the toughest to learn.

You're cruising downstream in moderately fast water on Georgia's magical, brooding Ogeechee River. You pop around a corner—and there are some tight ones!—and there's a tree down across the river. And I mean across the river! There might be a little sneak passage on the far end; there almost always is. But you were checking out the river swamp on one side and the hundred foot high hardwood bluff on the other side of the river, and all of a sudden, there's this tree, and you'd best do something about missing it. (Running into a downed

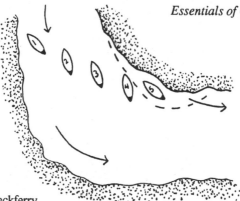

Figure 8-1 The Backferry

tree is bad news. You can dump the boat and the current can sweep you into the tree but not you through the tree. It's called a "strainer," and it's great if you have gills. But you don't.) You could sideslip, but you'd still be moving downstream. You could hang a hard right, but the current might drive you into the tree. Or you can hang the canoe in the current, set up the proper angle of the canoe to the current, and scoot across the river like a water bug and find that narrow slot around the tree on the far side.

How to do it? Tough to explain; there are a lot of variables, like the speed of the current and the design of your canoe. But, if you set your canoe at about a 10-20 degree angle to the direction of the current, with the stern backpaddling on the downstream side of the canoe and the bow on the upstream, and balance the power of your strokes to the speed of the current, you're good to go. Add a little finesse to this, and lean the boat downstream to keep the big, bad current from piling up on the up stream side and wedging the canoe over, and you'll really be good to go!

The "upstream ferry" is a move generally associated with whitewater, but for those of us who view upstream paddling against a stiff current as an art form that (1) makes you feel good about yourself, (2) gets you to places that you might not otherwise get to, and (3) obviates the need for a shuttle, so you can paddle by yourself, it's a necessary part of the armamentarium.

There's really no difference between an upstream ferry and a downstream ferry except that your canoe is going upstream current, depending on current speed and hull design. the stern is still on the downstream side, to keep the paddle from being swept under the fat part of the canoe, and the bow on the upstream side. You're still leaning a bit downstream. And you still go from one side of the river to the

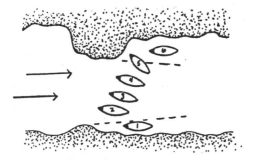

Figure 8-2 The Upstream Ferry.

other with the alacrity of a water bug.

You can practice this anywhere there's moving water. It's neat. It's fun. It will feel funny the first few times you do it, because your eyes will play some tricks on you. It almost makes some people light-headed the first few times they do it. But once you've mastered the upstream and downstream ferries, you've bought yourself a huge chunk of freedom of the river.

Was there a narrow slot on the far end of that tree across the Ogeechee? Gee, I don't remember. You'd best go down and check it out for yourself—after you've had breakfast at Judy's Cafe in Millen, Georgia.

Upstream Paddling

Here's where you use a lot of the strokes you've learned, and use them powerfully. And wisely, too. The upstream ferry is a necessity, so you can slide from side to side and find the path of least resistance. Stern draws and pushaways are necessary to slip sideways into the current from an eddy. High and low braces, both static and active, are necessary, because this is moving water, and it exerts surprising force on your canoe. And you'd best be able to paddle forward with power, switch sides without missing a beat, and work as a team without finding fault with each other.

You need not be a Top Gun candidate to look at a fast-moving river (not a complex whitewater river) and see where the slower-moving water is. It's downstream of obstructions. It's along the shoreline, more so to the inside of a bend than the outside, but it's always there. It's downstream of rocks. If you're a trout angler (the word "fisherperson" doesn't make it!), the slower water is where you'd look for fish. Sometimes, if the river is fast enough, the slow-water stretches along the shoreline are actually flowing upstream. And if you can slip your canoe into those eddies, you can catch a great upstream ride. But it takes boat-handling skills to ferry back and forth, find an eddy here, and an eddy there, muscle upstream when you have to (and you will have to, sooner or later), pop into an eddy downstream of a big rock and catch a breather; oops, there's a better way, but we have to go downstream, catch another eddy, ferry across right up to the shore, and…. Hey, folks; that's fun!

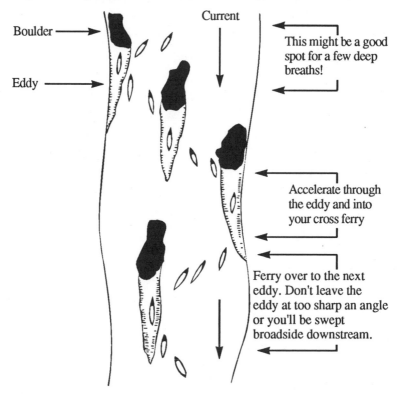

Boulder ⟶

Current

This might be a good spot for a few deep breaths!

Eddy ⟶

Accelerate through the eddy and into your cross ferry

Ferry over to the next eddy. Don't leave the eddy at too sharp an angle or you'll be swept broadside downstream.

Figure 8-3 Eddy Hopping on the Montreal

Turning
You can use the fact that current varies to help you turn the canoe with surprisingly little effort. In fact, you can use the current to make a long, lean, mean tourer fairly dance down a twisty little stream while your clueless friends are picking themselves out of the weeds.

Interlude
Story time! Years ago, my friend Dave Clayman paddled a touring kayak the length of the AuSable. While on the river, he met one

of the river patrol rangers, who mentioned something to the effect that there were a lot of bankers on the river yesterday. Dave asked if there was a convention, something like the A.B.A. or the Michigan Banker's Association. The ranger said that this wasn't the case. But there were a lot of canoeists who couldn't turn their craft in this fast-flowing world class trout stream, and when they came to a turn in the river, they ran into the bank. The current spun them around, and they drifted downstream to the next turn, where they again hit the bank and the current turned them. "'Round here, we call them 'bankers,' eh?" said the ranger, and slipped upstream in his solo canoe.

There's the lesson. Poke the nose of the canoe into a part of the stream that's moving slower than the slug of water you're riding, plant a static draw into the water, and see how fast the current will swing the canoe around! It's great fun, and is helped immeasurable if the stern

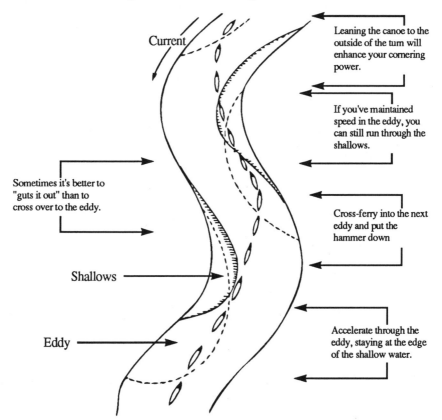

Figure 8-4 Upstream on the AuSable

paddler leans downstream and is ready with a low brace. (Lean upstream and all the braces in the world won't help.) Find enough current differential, such as you might find behind a big rock or on the inside of a sharp turn, and the stern paddler will feel like he or she's playing "crack the whip" on skates. This, simply stated, is the way you enter an eddy. River runners call it "eddying out." And you can play minor variations in current speed to help to turn on any stream. Play it just right, and nobody will figure out how you're doing it!

To get out of the eddy and back on downstream, enter the current with the canoe at a 45 degree angle to the current, bow on the (eventual) downstream side, stern upstream. Drive briskly across the eddyline, with the bow leaning downstream and putting in a static draw. The boat and the bow paddle will be caught up by the current, and the boat will swing rapidly downstream. Call a switch just as the stern paddler crosses the eddyline (to keep the stern's paddle from being swept under the boat), pour on the power, and go. You've just done a "peel-out!" Wasn't that fun?

Classical whitewater technique is a bit cleaner, and may be the only excuse for a touring paddler to learn a cross-bow maneuver, which keeps the stern on the downstream side in a better position to brace. Check out the sketch and play, play, play!

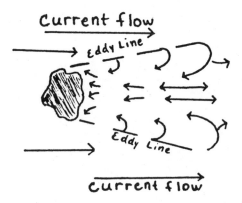

Figure 8-5 An Eddy Behind A Rock

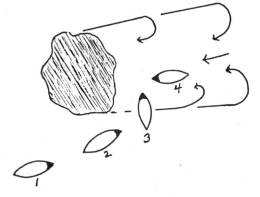

Figure 8-6 Entering An Eddy

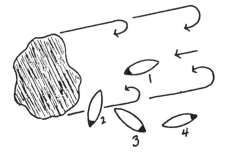

Figure 8-7 Leaving An Eddy

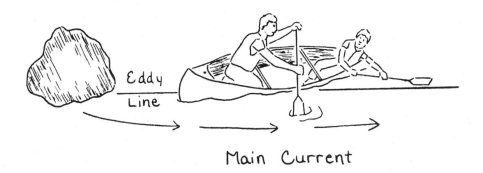

Figure 8-8 One Situation Where A Cross-Bow Maneuver Is Useful.

Figure 8-9 Basic River Strategy

TAKEOUT

If there's a secret all paddlers share, it's this. All paddling is great paddling, and any watercourse deep enough to float a boat is great paddling water.

So, now you know something about paddling an open canoe with another person, utilizing a style called North American Touring Technique. And I kept the promise I made at the beginning of the book, that I wouldn't use that overwrought phrase again until the last chapter.

This is it. The music ain't goin' round again, so if you want to dance, now's the time. I hope this little book tempts you to dance with your partner in a canoe. I hope it gets you so stoked on paddling that you get off your patio furniture and spend those magical twilight hours on some local waterway every night. I hope it gets you so revved up that you try other kinds of canoeing and other kinds of canoes. They're there; maneuverable little sport tandems, incredibly responsive whitewater boats, big trippers that can swallow a month's worth of gear, lean, mean racing machines. They're there for solo paddlers too. It doesn't matter what you like to do, the boats are there to do it.

And I hope you don't neglect kayaks, either. They too come in all sizes and shapes, from long, lean sea tourers to nimble whitewater play boats and those incredible little craft called squirt boats, that are as at home under the water as on the surface. Now, that's talking new dimensions in paddling!

And, when you're zipping around on the water somewhere, feeling your muscles working, hearing a good hull carving through the water with the sound of silk being torn, sensing and delighting in your skill of your partner, caressing the shaft and the grip of your paddle as you drive into it, let the boat glide for a bit. Let the birds come back to the forest canopy. Watch the slantwise sunlight flicker on the ripples of your passing. Feel your blood moving. Dip up a handful of water and splash it on your face, and enjoy the tiny chill it brings. Celebrate sensation. Celebrate living. Celebrate the movement of the boat.

Because it is said that only those who move will die. But paddlers know that those who do not move are dead already.

INDEX